Vertical Gardening For Beginners:

How to Grow and Harvest Plants, Vegetables and Fruits in Small Spaces

By

Erin Morrow

Table of Contents

Introduction 5

Chapter 1. The Good About Gardening 7

Chapter 2. Advantages of Vertical Gardening 10

Chapter 3. Misconceptions and Facts 14

Chapter 4. What Plants are Best to Grow Vertically? 16

Chapter 5. Building The Garden 18

Chapter 6. Watering 27

Final Words 30

Thank You Page 31

Vertical Gardening For Beginners: How to Grow and Harvest Plants, Vegetables and Fruits in Small Spaces

By Erin Morrow

© Copyright 2015 Erin Morrow

Reproduction or translation of any part of this work beyond that permitted by section 107 or 108 of the 1976 United States Copyright Act without permission of the copyright owner is unlawful. Requests for permission or further information should be addressed to the author.

This publication is designed to provide accurate and authoritative information in regard to the subject matter covered. This work is sold with the understanding that the publisher is not engaged in rendering legal, accounting, or other professional services. If legal advice or other expert assistance is required, the services of a competent professional person should be sought.

First Published, 2015

Printed in the United States of America

Introduction

Being a so-called green thumb is said to be something that can be learned through due exposure, experience, research, and observation, among others. You can always, during your free time, do some practicing, observe and even get coaching from someone who has been doing it at least longer than you have tried. Aside from time, and probably money, lack of space has been listed among the top reasons why people do not maintain a garden.

People in the rural areas generally have the edge in keeping a garden adjacent or even within their houses, as mostly, those places are not as crowded as those in the cities, where every square meter of a condominium unit is worth your bank account, and the convenience of your car becomes more of a priority if there is extra space within your property. But if you are socioeconomically an average inhabitant of one the busiest parts of the world, chances are that you do not have the luxury of 1) time to spend in your garden, and 2) space to lay your plants in.

Now you have no excuse. Pragmatists, and probably minimalists have already figured out how to make use of that bare wall at your house, paving the way to contributing solution to the lack of greens in the city due lack of space, secondary to congestion. Even without being skillfully, financially or physically ready to start gardening to the fullest, you can 'begin' taking your first steps to your jumpstart. One of the first few moves you may be able to take at anytime is to look into the benefits you can get out of starting a garden of your own. This is considered an initial step towards the end, as knowing how something could be beneficial to you encourages you to move closer to the attainment of your objectives.

Chapter 1. The Good About Gardening

One of the good things about engaging in nature-loving activities is that you involve yourself in a universal advocacy even without having to know it. Your inexplicable connection to 'mother nature' is a manifestation of your membership in a greater ecosystem, in which you have a shared responsibility with equal members. Your calling to join the force in growing more plants, whether to have your own source of nourishment, or to merely beautify your surroundings, is something, which when you respond to is a legacy in itself – you are contributing something significant for the future.

Another benefit of gardening, is that it is a therapy on its own. In the same way as music can heal, and arts can elicit relaxation, your engagement with the auspices of nature is something that can puts you in a state of tranquility, if you allow it to. Only certain theories may be attempting to prove this, but if you test the phenomenon by experiencing it yourself, you will be able to appreciate that which may be unfathomable, indeed.

The general advantage of this endeavor is simply good health. Being exposed to nature, deliberately working with nature, engaging in a kind of exercise, and also ingesting the products of nature, are healthy activities that helps achieve a certain degree of what is called homeostasis, meaning, the state of equilibrium among the different elements of yourself.

Physiologically and pathologically, the act of gardening is believed to reduce your stress levels, thereby increasing the quality of your health at all the dimensions of the human being. Stress, being said to be what causes most forms of discomforts that you could feel, could change your mood, decrease your level of enthusiasm, induce irritability, pain and heart attacks, and aggravates pre-existing conditions. One good thing about gardening is that you get to have a source of good vibes from the sense of fulfillment you get for being productive, while maintaining a readily available source of a green (or even colorful) scenery for your eyes.

Financially, having a garden with the wisely chosen plants can help you earn some bucks, if you work on it. If you are growing edible plants, it would also help you save some money from grocery shopping. If you eventually get to master the art of gardening, you may also earn from consultations, write-ups and other types of services. Indeed this can help boost not only your financial health, but also your sense of fulfillment.

Chapter 2. Advantages of Vertical Gardening

Aside from the obvious that vertical gardening saves you a significant amount of space, if not creates a planting space for you, there are much more additional benefits in growing your plants up. Doing so saves you money from the usual budget on the basic components of gardening, rids you of undesirable elements, provides your plants better ventilation, and makes you utilize your creative juices.

Saving money and energy. Doing your plants upright is said to be synonymous to needing less water, less fertilizers, less work and less worry. Aside from the financial aspect it so sweetly pampers, it also provides an opportunity for beginning gardeners to begin well, finding ease in doing plants, getting encouraged to stick with the deed, thus giving them a good vision of success in gardening, despite limited gardening spaces. The perks that saving both money and energy so radiate that they sometimes become translated into more tangible manifestations of what others may call 'good vibes' or 'positive aura'. Being able to save on two of the things that are usually wasted in life nowadays also results to a feeling of productivity and a sense of fulfillment, making you possibly want to keep repeating what it is that evoked such effect.

Easier riddance of unwanted elements. If you have done some horizontal gardening or simply planting in the past, you have probably encountered weeds, pests, and diseases. These are well-known hindrances to healthy thriving of plants from the ground or beds. You probably have experienced weeding all the bare soil areas, in order to keep your area clean and healthy. Although a normal part of conventional gardening, it indeed strips you of your energy – that which you could have spent appreciating the fruits, and smelling the flowers. The good news, however, is that having to weed your soil areas in vertical gardening, is not usually a 'normal' thing, as you often begin gardening with weed-free bagged soil. In case there are any incidents of weeds sprouting out of the soil at all, it will just be fewer weeds you will encounter. Such possibility can be considered unusual, because in case one or two weeds sneak in, they can easily be plucked out of the area in a while. You are moreover working with less soil surface so plants fill in and crowd out weeds.

Better air circulation. Wondering why there are less trouble with pests and disease in this kind of gardening, along with weeds? The answer is simple. Because of the location of plants, which is obviously off the ground, those that are grown upward receive better air circulation around the foliage, leading to the reduction of problems encountered with pests and disease. Since resolution in the supposed problematic existence of pests and disease in the gardening area seems to be present, it may be concluded that better air circulation yields to healthier plants, as evidenced by their strength, as well as unblemished produce. Since physical contact of plants with soil and soil-borne diseases are limited in vertical gardening, your plants are more taken care of, just by your means of growing them vertically.

Your creativity. Given your seemingly limited space and resources to start and maintain a garden, especially if you are in an urban area, your desire to have one, plus knowledge you can readily research, can bring your ideas of your vertical garden to topnotch designs that will speak of you and only you. You can work out on a functional vertical system or rather, a more architectural look to your garden. From limited resources, you can start with your creative imagination, and just allow the realization of your creative juices to be embodied in your soon-to-be magnum opus: your very own garden. Having such creativity harnessed for the purpose of worthwhile undertakings such as gardening also provides a person with a good intrapersonal experience. Being in a situation where you stare at a bare wall, then make ways to utilize it by accessorizing it with eye-soothing greens and other relaxing colors, arranging the items according to your creative preference, can send you a taste of fulfillment, for allowing your creative pleasures to turn your actions into something that is not only personally productive, but also environmentally responsible.

Chapter 3. Misconceptions and Facts

There are many misconceptions existing about gardening. Some, if not most people tend to view the garden – vegetable or otherwise, as long rows of straggly plants. For instance, if you ask a child to draw a garden, chances are that he or she would illustrate on with trees, shrubs, and other plants growing from the ground. While container gardening may have also been as popular already, having a plant hanged in such an illustration is quite unlikely. In short, people have long had the idea notion that plants grow from the ground.

However, how the limitations of urban living has compelled people like you to find ways to go about life as it can only be at a given circumstance, is astounding. It has indeed reached the point of adjusting to the environment in terms of trying to be healthy, productive and safe. People have started to learn growing their own fresh food in such a way that the very limited lifestyle they have can allow it. As more and more people have been finding ways to live as holistically healthy as possible, they keep finding ways to make it more and more improved.

However, with the lack of perceived need of other people who perhaps have vast lands, no interest with planting or no interest with anything related to it, none among them may have had the opportunity to appreciate the innovation just yet.

Chapter 4. What Plants are Best to Grow Vertically?

However, the most common trend has been planting edible plants, or otherwise known as food or vegetable gardening. Food gardening has been perceived to be the most practical type of gardening today, as people tend to be more and more conscious of their health. By planting their own veggies, fruits and herbs, they are sure that the source of their nourishment is indeed safe – that is, safe.

For most practical vertical gardeners, vegetable gardening is best applied in vertical growing of plants. Another incorporated principle on gardening is container gardening, in which plants are grown in pots, bins, even tires, or any other container, thus are not directly planted on the grounds. Examples of plants that can be grown in a containers are what they call, 'vertically challenged vegetables' such as lettuce, carrots, eggplants, potatoes, peppers, radishes, and spinach. These can all be grown vertically in containers. Moreover, for naturally vining types of vegetables, containers are hardly used, as their vertical growth is well-facilitated by the system of other types of vertical gardening. Examples of vining types are: peas, cucumbers, tomatoes, summer and winter squashes, such as small pumpkins.

Chapter 5. Building The Garden

If you want to build a vertical vegetable garden, the following are things you cannot fail to consider.

Where to build

How much space you have is one primary question to be entertained in considering building a vertical garden. Where you intend to build it is another you have to decide on. A usual follow-up is whether or not you have a bare wall? If you do, perfect. You got your space.

Next to consider in terms of location is sunlight. Remember that that most vegetables require at least 4 hours of sun exposure. In order for you to go strategic with your location, pick the wall that faces south to provide your plants with a significant amount of light. In case you live in an area surrounded by other buildings, your balcony may be usually shaded. This does not necessarily disqualify you from gardening up; in fact, you may just choose your plants appropriately. Leafy vegetables like cabbage, lettuce, and other greens, do well with minimal sunlight, which makes them a great fit for shady areas.

What to build: The easy types

Trellises that are purchased are usually what most people think of when asked about vining plants. However, there are other types you can use for you climber plants, such as use nets, fences, gates, chicken wire, frames, ladders, string on pole, and more.

Trellises. Trellises are frames which are composed of elongated pieces of wood, crossing each other. They can be utilized to hold straggling crops, or what may be more understood as vine plants.

Building a garden trellis is very easy and doable if you have time to do it. If not, there are readily available frames that would be perfect for your green wall. But in case you have the time and the willingness to build one, consider situating them along the north side of your garden to prevent shading. That is, if you have other plants. Consider too, to secure your frames in order to keep them safe from the wind, holding the plants' weight. This can be done by sinking your posts around 24 inches deep. That is, if there is a way to sink them.

If you want to build a simple "trellis roof", however, you are going to need four strong wooden poles, those which will serve as the frame's foundation to anchor the roof, and strong rectangular sticks to support the roof trellis and the plants. The wooden poles need to be cut into thinner ones, into about 25 pieces, considering that the area is considerably small, in order to allow the vines to weave themselves through freely, and for the gourd to hang down. This is also to be done intentionally so that other vegetables may grow underneath with enough sun to shine through. Next, with the help of your hammer and some strong 2 inch nails to secure the poles, you now have built your very own trellis.

Growing a vertical garden using a trellis enables you to save space, grow and harvest plants easily, provide shade for other plants, allow better circulation, and come up with a good-looking garden. As you venture into saving space, you get to produce much more vegetables with not much space occupied, that is, horizontally.

As it makes it easy to grow and harvest products, it also keeps the plants away from the ground, where insects, pests, diseases and weeds damage the plants. In harvesting, moreover, you need not break your spinal cord, trying to bend just to tend your crops. Having a trellis for a garden allows you ergonomic gardening, as you get to maintain and harvest at eye level. Aside from this very important ergonomic characteristic of vertical gardening, it also provides an aesthetic effect wherever it is situated. It allows a creation of what they say is a whole different dimension to your landscape.

Moreover, it tends to help protect plants that need some shade, allowing you to make use of whatever else space is available for others. It also provides good ventilation, something that your plants need alongside water and sunlight.

Containers. Vertical gardens are not limited to vining plants, as there are other ways to create that green wall. Almost every vegetable grown in a garden can work well as a container-grown plant. Most types of container can be utilized to grow vegetable plants. Old tubs, toy bins, gallon-sized coffee cans, and even a single boot can be implemented for growing crops as long as they provide adequate drainage. You may make use of hanging vegetables baskets, recycled bags and stacked pots in different colors, sizes and shapes, can all contain plants that don't climb.

Hanging baskets. Hanging baskets will look great on the patio, or even just on hangers. You can grow as many kinds of veggies in hanging baskets, especially those that sprawl. Peppers and tomatoes, as well as vines such as that of the sweet potato are said to be look good in hanging baskets. In growing anything in hanging baskets, it is important to keep them watered every day, because drying out is a consistent tendency of hanging baskets. This is even much truer during the dry seasons.

Shelves. Shelves are one of the excellent types of containers that can definitely be used in vertical gardening. It has the capacity to grow different variants of vegetables with the instant divisions, with the feature of a good (and hopefully reasonable) height. The vertical vegetable garden may be positioned in such a way that each plant gets to have sufficient sunlight at the same time. In case Mr. Sun is your best friend, you may give tomatoes, potatoes, beans, carrots, radishes and peppers the chance to thrive under the full sun they love in your vertical garden. Even vine crops, can be grown as long as the container is deep enough to accommodate them and proper staking is available.

What to plant.

What you should plant is what you can. It is even better if you can plant what you want to. If you are planting veggies, then plant what you want to eat. Of course, you should not fail to consider other factors that may be contributing to what limits or enhances you to choose what to grow, such as the time you can devote to tending your plants, the kind of work you have, especially if you are working away from home, your current gardening skills, your financial budget for necessary elements, the weather, the structure of your 'wall', and many others. Considering all these, it would still be most fulfilling to care for plants that will yield foods that will provide you and your family fresh nourishment.

When still considering gardening up, you can do one that contains what you can use in the kitchen, such as basic veggies. Some enthusiasts call this edible gardening. For a successful attempt on this, it is important that you have at least an initial list of what vegetables can feasibly do this. Read on.

Tomatoes. Tomatoes are said to be both fruits and vegetables. They are considered fruits, they say, when eaten as they are, but are vegetables because they are used for cooking. They are best grown under full sunlight, and from a loamy type of acidic soil. They may be planted using their seeds, or their transplants. In planting seeds, you should start indoors, where there is full sun and well-drained yet moist soil, for around 6 to 8 weeks. They are to be exposed to sunlight for no less than 6 hours of each day. On the 5th week, the soil must be tilled 12 inches deep, mixing aged manure or compost as fertilizer. After around seven days of hardening off the seedlings after last spring frost, move them outdoors. This is best done when the soil is warm.

Tomatoes can also be grown using a wire cage or a trellis. But because they like to throw themselves over their support, the cage is said to work best with tomatoes. To do this, you may insert a circular cage wire deep into the soiled ground surrounding your tomato plant. When using trellis, you have to tie it with ropes. This is not as easy as growing them in wire cages.

Cucumbers. Cucumbers are a good choice to grow because they grow very fast. Moreover, all their varieties also grow on vines. Lemon cucumbers, in particular, grow fast but the produce is not as big as typical cucumbers. Smaller cucumbers are good because they branch out more. Over time, they gently weave the vines in between the vertical surfaces of the trellis. They can be tied it in certain places to help them grow more while staying anchored.

Green beans. The numerous varieties of beans, such as green beans, sugar snap peas, and snow peas, all require a surface to climb. As they mature, these vines continue to climb, and the small thin structures they develop called tendrils, would clutch on to whatever they may be able to grasp as they move. Because of their lightness in weight, this kind of vegetables would work with a simple trellis, or even rope system.

Chapter 6. Watering

Alongside sunlight, air and nutrients from the soil, water keeps a plant alive and healthy. In fact water composes much of the entirety of a plant. A plant that is not watered enough, or is watered too much, is not okay either. Watering is said to have no hard or fast rules. There are several variables affecting the specific needs of a plant to be watered. Some of these are the type of plant, the soil, the temperature, and the season.

There have been several mechanisms by which the system of watering plants have been tried to improve to maximize efficiency. For one, a system that has been gaining popularity in its efforts to solve the dilemma on watering vertically grown plants what is called an automatic drip irrigation system. Because of the location, your plants are more prone to sun, air and wind, sun and air. Since drying out may be rather fast for them, watering regularly to maintain soil moisture is imperative. If you are using containers, moreover, you may utilize self-watering containers to achieve the same, in case you do not have the luxury of time to manually water them all the time.

Of course the abovementioned approaches are not of the conventional, as there are much simpler ways to water the plants, such as the use of much simpler materials. But in whichever approach you decide to employ, there are basic principles that are supposed to be maintained when watering your plants properly.

Where. First is to focus on the roots. The very thing to remember is that the roots are what absorb the nutrients and the water from the soil to the rest of the parts of the plant. Watering the plants by making the water run through the leaves is not proper watering, neither is it effective. The proper way to do it is to soak the soil just right.

When. Second is to water according the plant's need. Some technologies make use of automatic timers, which are indeed useful when programmed accordingly, as there may be other variables affecting the plants' needs, which may be beyond the device's automaticity.

How. Third thing to remember is to water deeply and meticulously. Know just how deep the roots of the plants you are tending are, so that you may know how much water you need to give them. Are you dealing with potted herbs? What about those leafy ones inside the shelf? And those flowery plants in the basket?

All in all, watering plants takes paying attention. You may have observed a gardener checked out a pot in the nursery, trying to feel if the soil inside the pot is moistened. Maybe you are wondering why she lifted the basket, seemingly trying to sense whether it's heavy enough, before pouring the water on its soil? It may seem difficult for a beginner to even imagine, but some people are just blessed to be able to easily figure out what to do to a plant by merely checking the soil if it 'feels right'. However, there are more obvious clues to check whether or not a plant needs water or not by keeping track of its characteristics, and when you're still beginning, there's always the label from the seeds' packaging.

Final Words

Being green thumb is not a requirement to grow any plant – whether it's on the ground, in a pot, of hanging on a wall. You need no 'unusual ability' just to get your hand working on growing any plant. It may take some time to learn and practice, but definitely being able to grow plants and maintain a vertical garden can be learned. Getting the hang of it may just be on its way, but it is around.

So, do you think you could have the green thumb, but not the wide land? No problem.

Thank You Page

I want to personally thank you for reading my book. I hope you found information in this book useful and I would be very grateful if you could leave your honest review about this book. I certainly want to thank you in advance for doing this.

If you have the time, you can check my other books too.

www.ingramcontent.com/pod-product-compliance
Lightning Source LLC
LaVergne TN
LVHW021747060526
838200LV00052B/3528